TEXTED LIES, WHISPERED TRUTHS

TERRI ANNE BROWNING

LONNIE DORIS

DISCLAIMER

This is not a work of fiction.
It is Jason Collier's narrative in his own words, written by
Terri Anne Browning and Lonnie Doris. All information
detailed in this book came directly from Jason Collier
himself. Most of it was already presented on social media by
others involved, while Jason remained quiet.
Now, you will hear his side of the story.
From the very beginning.

This story is true.
Some names have been changed to protect the privacy of others involved.

Dear Readers,

This is my story. These are my words and experiences. Thank you for reading my side of the story. Thank you Terri Anne and Lonnie for putting them on paper.

PREFACE

"The next time your man says he doesn't have time for you, remind him Jason Collier has time for a wife, four kids, two fiancées, being police chief, a ministry, a Pinterest page, two coffeepots, and seventeen girlfriends."

The moment I read that post on Facebook, I spat the drink of water I had just taken out of my mouth, my bed now soaked and my husband looking at me like I'd lost my mind at my seemingly unprovoked reaction. I wasn't normally so over-dramatic...

Okay, that's a lie. I am an author after all. There must be a law somewhere that says all authors must be overly dramatic in at least one aspect of their lives. My husband is an understanding man, and he puts up with my eccentricities. But I was taking a break after writing my newest book, *Her Shelter*, so he wasn't prepared for my sudden sputter that sprayed him and our freshly changed sheets with bottled water.

It was January 27, 2021, and I was decompressing in bed

after a full day of homeschooling three kids, dealing with a disabled dog, and basically trying to survive the continued self-enforced quarantine—because, hey, it's a fucking pandemic and I have a heart condition. My typical end of the day routine included scrolling through social media, more often than not, hoping to find a new book that may have recently released and which might hold my attention for more than 3.2 seconds.

That was when the post caught my attention. I'd seen a few people talking about some police chief and his many mistresses earlier in the day, but I'd kept scrolling because I honestly didn't know if they were talking about real-life people or some movie/sitcom that I was too busy and didn't have the attention span to focus on. Alas, it was very much reality, as I was soon to find out.

One of Lonnie's and my mutual friends shared a post, and it was the next thing I saw in my feed. Beyond curious—and noting the 500-plus comments on the picture that had been shared—I quickly fell down the Jason Collier rabbit hole, one that would keep me fascinated for the next two hours before I even lifted my head from my phone. During that time, I was sure my entire house could have caught fire, my children could have invented a cure for COVID while my Frenchies suddenly took up juggling, and I wouldn't have noticed or heard any of it.

As soon as I came up for air, I shared the same picture-post that was not just a rabbit hole but, in fact, a blazing dumpster fire. It had been roughly twenty-four hours since the post had first gone live, and already, it was reaching people worldwide. If I was going to be sucked into the whole Jason/Candie/Stephanie/Mr. Coffee drama, then those on my friends list were coming with me. (Not their real names. I have a little respect for people...sometimes. So, they've been renamed in an attempt to protect their privacy.) But hey, if you're reading this, you already know who they really are.

BECAUSE THEY TOLD YOU WHO THEY ARE!

To begin with, I was engrossed by the story. Woman catches boyfriend cheating through a mutual friend with his other girlfriend—fiancée? mistress?—and he has a wife? *Or so she was telling everyone.* Now others were coming forward, and it was looking more and more like a Lifetime Sunday Movie Special. I was already mapping out an entire series focused on the events, in which the group of women come together, become lifelong besties, learn to love themselves for who they really are, and then find true love. With separate men, mind you. They weren't going to do some weird sister-wives thing. I mean...I had to have more than one book in this series Lonnie and I were already plotting...

But then, in the background, we both noticed the stories weren't matching up. The red flags had my stomach turning, because it was all clicking in my head. Someone was sucking up all the attention, keeping herself in the spotlight, and seemingly not giving a damn that the more she egged on the drama, the more she was hurting those who were blameless in this entire fiasco. Jason's children were being dragged into the mess, and I began to pull away from the drama.

What had become, to me, a few hours of reading entertainment was actually the crash and burn of someone's life. Admittedly, I wasn't all that worried about how Jason Collier was holding up. As an outsider looking in, I couldn't find any sympathy for the man, when he had brought all of this upon himself.

His children? They were the innocents, the ones who hadn't asked for any of this drama to overtake and upend their lives, but that was exactly what was happening. And as I continued to watch—albeit from more of a distance at this point—I saw the damage someone seemed to enjoy inflicting as they destroyed these children's lives with each post and interview she participated in.

Lonnie, who was still trapped within the flames of the dumpster fire we had both fallen into, reached out to Jason, and it was then that I reminded myself there are always three sides to every story.

His.

Hers.

And somewhere, mixed into all of the bullshit from either side, the truth.

Lonnie convinced me that we needed to give Jason a voice, and after some internal struggling, I agreed. Not because of him, but because of the injustice, the pain and humiliation others were inflicting—apparently without remorse—on those who were the true innocents and victims in this train wreck.

We knew that someone would tell Jason's story. Whether it was us or some tabloid or even a more reputable magazine. There was no stopping that train, I don't care what anyone says. But at least this way, we knew what would be printed, and we could ensure the children would be taken care of with the majority of any proceeds.

This is Jason's truth. In his own words. Lonnie and I have worked together to present to you a variation of the story you were so wrapped up in. Because, admit it. You fell down that rabbit hole right along with us back in January. It's why you're reading this now.

Is it fucked up?

Definitely.

Do I condone what he did?

No! No, a million times no—see, I'm back to being over-dramatic. Sigh.

But does he deserve to have his story told?

Well, fuck, people. Wouldn't you want your story told if given the chance?

1

From the City of Stinnett, Texas, Facebook Page
"Facebook User" *doesn't recommend* **City of Stinnett**.
Jan 26 at 10:40 AM

"Chief Jason Collier is living a double/triple life. I was his girlfriend until yesterday. He lied to me and presented me with fake annulment documents when I found out he was married. I also found out about a 2nd girlfriend, Stephanie, last night. He has lied to us, our children, and asked us both to marry him. He is a poor representative of your town. He would also visit me in Amarillo when he was on shift. We just returned from vacation in Taos on Sunday—meanwhile, his other GF was told he was on work assignment in Portland, OR."

THAT POST WAS SUDDENLY WORLDWIDE NEWS, AND I, JASON Brent Collier, at the age of forty-one, was now the meme that was taking over the internet. Only the day before, it was still Bernie Sanders, sitting in that chair at President Biden's inauguration, looking chilled to the bone in his winter coat and mittens. Social media was overrun with people joking that they thought dear old Bernie would be the meme that "Brought America Together Again," but apparently it was me. Pictures of me and coffeepots, me and a cardboard bride in her wedding dress with the face cut out so that tourists could add their own, not to mention the songs I was now featured in on not only Facebook, but YouTube as well.

People who didn't know me were making timelines of all the women I was supposedly dating, engaged to, or even reportedly married to and had a child with. Some of these people, I didn't even know...

But unfortunately, several of them I did, in fact, know.

Not just in passing, but in the biblical sense.

Because I wasn't innocent in the chaos that was now taking over my life after a single vindictive post placed on the Facebook page for the City of Stinnett, Texas, where I was the police chief. I had a moment of insanity—admittedly, that moment evolved into several months—but the man the world was currently tearing apart limb from limb wasn't the real me.

I was the shy, quiet boy who grew up in Hereford, Texas, "Beef Capital of the World," which was located about forty-eight miles southwest of Amarillo. My dad, Jerry, was a Vietnam War veteran and owned a full-service gas station where I had my first job at the age of seven, pumping gas. And when I was tall enough, I started doing oil changes and washing the cars that came in for service.

He and my mom, Carole, were married in April of 1970, and I was their second son. Everyone respected them and knew my brother and me because we worked at the station. In the 1990s, they sold the station and started a car dealership. When they bought vehicles at auctions, I would travel with a group of older men, and we would drive the cars back. I had several other small jobs after that, even learned how to weld from my cousin, but I always knew I wanted to be a cop.

Working at the gas station, seeing the cops come in for service, I fell in love with the cars and admired the respect the officers got from others in our community. While I was in high school, I went through jailer's school, and afterward, I worked for a while at the Potter County Jail. I was never promoted, but I was steadily given more and more responsibilities.

At the age of twenty-one, I attended the Panhandle Regional Police Academy through Amarillo College, while still working full time. I would work the night shift then go to school from eight-to-five each day. I got little sleep during that time, but it was worth it because I graduated quicker than if I would have attended the night classes at the academy.

I took the state test and passed before getting a job offer from Carson County, where I became a deputy sheriff. After catching the eye of Rob Roach at the Panhandle Police Department, I was recruited and I switched jobs. They paid more at Panhandle, and I was able to receive more training. My police chief, Loren Brand, was from Chicago and retired in 2020 as sheriff of Carson County. I had so much respect and learned a great deal while working with him. When Chief Brand moved up, Rob became the chief of police, and I was promoted to the training officer.

My career was advancing more and more with each passing year. I loved my job and getting to serve and help those in the community where I lived.

It was my personal life where things got clouded.

2

_____

IN EARLY 2001, WHILE I WAS STILL WORKING FOR POTTER County Jail and attending the police academy, I met my first wife, M. She worked at the jail with me. The moment I saw her, I was instantly attracted. But having been shy my entire life, I knew talking to her was out of the question. Our coworkers would laugh at the two of us, because any time I would see her coming, I would immediately turn and practically run in the opposite direction.

During our lunch hour one night, I watched from across the room as she ate her meal. She was licking a spoon, and as I stared, she happened to glance over at me. My blush probably could have lit up the room, I turned so red. Later, when I finally got up the courage to talk to her and ask her out, she gave me a plastic spoon. "I like you," was written on it, and I held on to that memento.

Our relationship progressed, and I soon couldn't imagine my life without her. We went on vacation together to Vegas, and we were so enamored of each other, I think everyone assumed we would come home married and were shocked when we didn't.

Not long after that vacation, I bought a ring. For a while, I tried to plan how to propose, wanting to make it romantic and special, but I just couldn't hold it in. One night, she came over, and I busted out the ring and blurted out the proposal. Without hesitation, she said yes.

We moved in together, and when I began working for Carson County, she followed and worked as one of the dispatchers. The running joke with everyone was that she got to tell me where to go and what to do both at home and at work.

In July of 2001, we got married. By October of 2003, we welcomed our first child, a daughter. My girl is incredibly smart and beautiful, and I am beyond proud of all that she has already accomplished in life. She works hard in school and sports, and she plans on becoming a nurse.

When my daughter was still very young, we found out my mom was sick. She was the type of person who didn't go to the doctor for any reason. Maybe it was her generation, but I could never remember her or Dad speaking openly about...well, anything, but definitely not their health. By the time they found her cervical cancer, it was too late for treatment. It was her request to have hospice come in, and for weeks, we all waited for the call from Dad that it was her time.

It's hard to remember those moments because I was a true momma's boy, while my brother was closer to our father. Saying goodbye to my mother was one of the hardest things I've ever had to do. One evening, Dad called and said her time was coming fast.

That night, I sat by her bed and held her hand. She must have been dreaming and not quite in her right mind. Because of the cancer, she couldn't even close her eyes, but she kept telling me about when she was a little girl and riding horses. I read her the entire book of Solomon, and as the night went on, I told her it was okay for her to let go, to go on home.

Not long afterward, she took her last breath while I sat by her side.

It was harder for me than anyone could have understood. Not just losing her, but not being able to handle or express the grief that constantly seemed to live inside me.

It caused issues between M and me.

We separated. She went to live with her family with our daughter, and I moved in with my dad back in Hereford. During that time, we both started seeing other people. I met a woman who had a son. We talked for several months and even began dating, but I didn't want to be a part-time father. M and I decided to work things out and moved to Ralls, Texas, where I took my first police chief job.

Life went on. My marriage wasn't perfect; we had our issues—mainly money and how we handled our finances— and then later on, her parents became a problem. In 2010, while she was pregnant with our son, we moved to Pampa, Texas, and we bought our home in March of 2011. Mostly, the move was to be closer to my dad, but we lost him in July of that same year.

Losing one parent is hard, but losing both is agony.

I didn't know how to work through my grief, and it was all starting to build up inside me.

The loss once again put a strain on my marriage.

3

My weight was something I always struggled with. All my life, I was simply a big boy. But I was getting older, heavier, and frankly, I was miserable. At 430 pounds, I had no energy. And I knew if I wanted to live long enough to get the chance to walk my daughter down the aisle, see my son grow up, and hopefully, one day, hold my grandchildren, then I needed to make a change.

In October of 2014, I had weight loss surgery.

For anyone who doesn't know about bariatric, or weight loss, surgery, there are several different types. Gastric bypass (Roux-en-Y Gastric Bypass), sleeve gastrectomy, adjustable gastric band, and the biliopancreatic diversion with duodenal switch (BPD/DS).

For me, I went with the sleeve. It is a laparoscopic surgery in which about eighty percent of the stomach is removed. The remaining portion is a tubular pouch, and it is basically the shape and size of a banana. The new pouch that became my stomach held less, helping me to consume lower amounts of food and, of course, fewer calories. It more or less enforced portion control.

Once I had my surgery and my doctor released me to start working out, I lived in the gym. I worked out every day, and the weight just seemed to melt off me. I lost a total of 180 pounds.

Before surgery, you have requirements you have to fulfill before the doctor will do the procedure. Each state and, I assume, each doctor is different, but I don't remember it being too complicated. I think the most invasive thing I had to do was talk to a therapist, and that was accomplished by phone. The entire call lasted maybe fifteen to thirty minutes.

What they don't tell you when you have this surgery is how much your mental health is affected. I wasn't prepared for the attention I was suddenly getting as more and more of the weight fell off.

They don't tell you the statistics of the divorce rate for those who have bariatric surgery. I didn't know that up to forty-one percent of patients are more likely to get divorced within four years of having the procedure. Some states or doctors make you do couples therapy if you're married because this can put a strain on your marriage. At the time, I didn't know that, and it wasn't a part of my requirements to get surgery. I should have gone to group sessions or at the least spoken with other patients. No matter which surgery a person gets, each one has the same strong, life-altering effect.

As bariatric patients, we don't see ourselves losing the weight until it's so drastic that, one day, we look in the mirror, and we see an entirely new person staring back at us. And that messes with a person's mind on a totally different level than most people can comprehend.

Suddenly, I was getting attention. People were complimenting me, telling me how good I looked, noticing me for the first time. It felt good.

I won't make excuses and say my weight loss surgery was

why my life later turned into such a disaster. Having the gastric sleeve didn't make me do the things I did. It didn't put a gun to my head and force me to cheat on my wife or to lie to everyone in my life.

But if I had known the mental changes it would cause, I might have made a different decision. Looking back on it now, I ask myself, *Was the surgery worth it?*

Health-wise, yes. Definitely.

But in other aspects of my life, when I consider the emotional pain I've put not only myself, but those I love the most, through …

No. I honestly don't think it was.

4

Warning: This chapter may be graphic for some readers.

THE MENTAL CHALLENGES I WAS ENDURING FOLLOWING MY gastric sleeve procedure were nothing compared to what happened January 6, 2015—one of the worst moments in my career, and one that will live with me forever. It was a night-mare every police officer fears having to face, but is the potential reality we have to prepare ourselves for every time we leave our homes.

I was working at the Pampa Police Department at the time as a detective. A fellow officer and I were called out to a domestic disturbance with two other officers. Shots had already been reported being fired, and the suspect was refusing to come out of the house. The suspect was someone we were well acquainted with since he was a meth user. The night before, he'd spent his time beating his girlfriend. The only reason he'd stopped when he did was because their child needed to be fed.

Thankfully, the girlfriend had been able to get out of the

house before we arrived. But she and her friends were attempting to collect her things, which was why the suspect locked himself in the house and started shooting.

At first, I was busy directing traffic away from that part of the street, but soon, I was motioned to put on my vest and come assist. We tried to get the suspect to come out, but no one would answer, and after being advised how to proceed, we broke down the door and quickly cleared the front of the house.

With only two rooms left, my heart was pounding as I went into one with an officer, and the two other officers went into the other room. Just as I entered the room, I heard the unmistakable sound of the blast from a shotgun.

The officer I was with and I rushed toward the noise.

One officer was lying on the floor bleeding, while his partner was trapped in a corner, shouting into his radio, "Shots fired! Shots fired! Officer down!"

The suspect was hiding in the closet with a 12-gauge pressed to the door. The bullet had caught the officer in the face, taking off the lower left side of his jaw.

My partner and I reacted quickly. Call it adrenaline or all the working out I'd been doing since my surgery, but I picked up my fellow officer by his vest with one hand while my partner grabbed his feet, and we pulled him out of the room.

But we still had an officer trapped inside with the suspect. While my partner began administering lifesaving first aid to the injured officer, I went back and drew fire so his partner could get out. But the entire time I was pulling the suspect's attention to me, all I could really see and think about was my friend's jaw, lying on the floor.

Thankfully, he survived the shooting, but the four of us who were there that day were never really the same after that.

They say situations like that bring those involved closer together. That wasn't the case with us. Instead, it made us all drift apart.

I still suffer from PTSD because of that day.

5

CALL IT UNHEALTHY, BUT I HAVE A CONSTANT NEED FOR sexual affection.

And that need wasn't always something my first wife could meet.

The pain of losing my dad, on top of my mental health challenges following the shooting, put even more pressure on our marriage. I was working not only as a police officer, but also at Sears and even for Coke, stocking shelves in local stores, all while still continuing to work out at the gym most days. At home, there was a rift between M and me, and I was almost thankful for the extra work I had to do to keep up with the bills and the other expenses that life throws at a person.

Money was stable but tight following my surgery, other bills, and our daughter playing travel softball, which I also coached. But the biggest strain in our relationship was caused by her parents. Her mother was addicted to prescription drugs, and her father was a lifelong alcoholic, and he later turned to prescription drugs as well.

I felt like we couldn't go anywhere without getting a courtesy call from the local police, letting me know the cops were going to my in-laws' home or an ambulance was picking someone up from their residence because of their drug use. We never seemed to have any time to ourselves, time that was just for us. And that distance between us only seemed to increase.

In April of 2015, I brought up the subject of my wife and I having an open relationship. At first, she was hesitant, but the more I brought it up and pushed, the more she seemed willing to try. We started meeting people who shared our interests and going out to social gatherings with them.

The first party we attended was the night I met my second wife, O, for the first time. During the night, my cell phone went off, and M and I went out to the driveway to take the call. It was the dispatcher, once again letting me know that an ambulance was going to my in-laws' home. I was frustrated and angry, but I didn't want to leave. I felt like they had already ruined so much for us, and I wasn't willing to let them mess up this night.

As I tried to open the front door to reenter the party, I found it was locked, so I knocked. After a few moments, it opened, and that was when I saw *her* for the first time.

With one look at her, I felt something inside of me shift. When I met my first wife, there was instant attraction, but what I felt for her was more of a puppy-love infatuation in comparison to how I reacted to that first interaction with O.

There she stood looking at us, and I couldn't help smiling.

Later, when we talked about that moment, she told me that when I smiled at her, she knew she was in trouble.

In this new group of friends, M and I were the fresh blood, and we got lots of attention, but my eye had already been caught. That quickly, this woman changed my life.

A few days following the party, I found her on Facebook and friended her. After talking for a short while, we decided to go on a double date with our spouses. Once we had dinner, we ended up at a strip club. At the time, M didn't get along with O's husband, but that didn't stop the two of us from getting to know each other.

That night, I realized there wasn't just an instant attraction between me and the woman who would become my second wife. There was an immediate emotional attachment forming as well for both of us, and we decided to take our date back to her house. But before we could leave, her daughter called to say she was coming home early from a friend's house, and our plans were put on hold.

Disappointed, I didn't know what to do. I wanted to kiss her, make any move, really, but my shyness got in the way. She surprised me when she pushed me up against the building and kissed me, letting me know that everything I was feeling, she was feeling too.

At the end of the night, we went our separate ways with our spouses, but we stayed in contact, continuing to talk regularly.

6

OVER THE NEXT FEW WEEKS, I LEARNED MORE AND MORE about O.

She was coming to the end of her second marriage. Her first husband, who was also the father of her two children, had been both emotionally and physically abusive. The man she was married to at that point in time was...for want of a better word, weird. M didn't like him, so that made it impossible for the four of us to have a relationship, but that didn't stop me from wanting to be with O.

At another party, O and I decided it was going to be "our night." The party was held at the same house as the first party M and I attended, and we were also celebrating the host's birthday. All I could remember as the night seemed to drag on was thinking, "Hurry up and open your presents. Hurry. Up!"

As soon as the last present was opened, I grabbed O, and we disappeared into one of the bedrooms upstairs.

After that night, our relationship started building.

I knew I had to make a decision. M and I were still technically trying to keep our marriage together, but my heart was somewhere else. While I was dating, so was she, but she was also willing to work on our marriage.

When I realized I was in love with O, I decided to move out. It wasn't fair to M to think there was hope for us when my emotions were too far gone for someone else.

During this time, I was going through training to prepare me to take over as police chief of Pampa since the chief at the time was getting ready to retire. I'd been selected to take his place, and for a few months, I would travel down to Dallas for a week at a time for training.

O flew to Tennessee for work during my second week of training, and while she was gone, I confessed to her, "I'm pretty sure I'm in love with you."

"I love you too," she admitted, and she promised me when she returned, she was going to tell her husband their marriage was over.

When she flew home, her husband met her at the airport in Dallas with her kids, and they had a family weekend together. But when they got back to their house, she told him it was over and she was moving out. For a while, she moved in with her parents and then her sister. I helped her pack and move in to her sister's house.

Because of how her first marriage ended, she always kept divorce documents and decree templates on her computer. She even helped out a few people at her work by printing off the paperwork for them. When it was time for her to file for her second divorce, she didn't even need a lawyer to handle it because she already had everything she needed.

M and I had separated, and I was living on my own, and O was out of her husband's house. Each morning, I would leave early for work and stop at Starbucks before I met up with her. Her favorite was a latte, no foam, two Sweet'N

Lows. Sometimes I would be late for work because I just didn't want to say goodbye to her in the mornings.

My third week of training in Dallas, I asked her to come down to visit me. We went to Billy Bob's in Fort Worth, and I felt like I was in my element. There was no shyness, no being uptight. There was just her and me.

It felt...magical.

But my own divorce didn't come without consequences. When my boss found out about our separation and that we were getting a divorce, it was decided I wasn't right for the chief of police position I'd been training for. They gave the job to someone else.

That stung because I'd already invested so much of myself, and I was excited to become the police chief.

7

Even though my career had suffered a setback, I felt like my romantic relationship was strong and going well.

But that changed in Christmas of 2015.

Since the birth of my daughter, I'd always been there on Christmas morning for her and then my son. Even though their mother and I were now divorced, I didn't want that to change. At least not yet. While I had a new love in my life, I was still friends with my ex-wife.

I lied to O and told her I was going home after spending Christmas Eve with her and her family. Instead, I went to M's house, and once the kids were in bed, I helped her put out the presents and set up for the next morning. She slept in her bed, and I took the couch.

Christmas morning was much the same as it always had been for us—the kids waking up early to open presents, having breakfast together. It was what we all wanted, and needed, after the chaos of 2015.

But after I left for the day, my ex took it upon herself to call O and let her know where I had spent the night. Even though she hadn't contested the divorce, she blamed the other woman for our marriage breaking up, and she had a moment of vindictiveness. In all honesty, neither of us was innocent in the demise of our relationship. But that morning, it must have hit her harder for some reason, and she made the call to be spiteful.

O broke up with me that night.

I knew I shouldn't have lied, but because I wanted that time with my kids on Christmas morning, I did it anyway. Part of me regretted it, but I'm not sure I would have done it differently.

For the next few weeks, I called O almost every day, asking her to give me another chance. But she wouldn't even pick up.

Then one day, out of the blue, my cell phone rang. I was doing bailiff work, and because I was in court and didn't recognize the number, I sent it to voice mail. When I listened to the message, I was blown away. It was O, asking how I was doing.

By some miracle, she was willing to give our relationship another go.

Slowly, we made an effort to get back on track. I told her I would give her as much time as she needed to learn to trust me again. I wanted to make us work, because I loved her.

Mother's Day of 2016 she had to go to Vegas for work, and she invited me to go with her. We stayed at the Paris casino, and that night over dinner, I proposed.

On September 3, 2016, we got married in a small western-themed ceremony in our backyard. She wore a white lace dress and cowboy boots, while I wore jeans and a starched white shirt. And I made the love of my life my wife.

8

I WAS RAISED IN THE LUTHERAN CHURCH, BUT GOING TO services wasn't something we did regularly.

When I married M, she talked me into going to Trinity Fellowship with her, where Jimmy Evans was and still is the pastor. He and his wife, Karen, started MarriageToday, which now reaches 680 million households across 200 countries through their television program.

The first time I went, everything about the way they worshiped, compared to what I was used to at the Lutheran church, scared me. I'd never been to a church where they raised their hands as they sang or prayed. I told M I didn't want to go back. Respectfully, she didn't force the issue. But a few months later, I had this urge to give it another chance and decided to return. That Sunday, Pastor Evans's sermon was titled, "Why People Raise Their Hands During Worship," and it all just clicked for me.

After that, I got more and more into the church, but when we started having problems within our marriage, I found myself drifting further and further away from God.

O was raised Catholic, though she hadn't ever really

embraced religion. But after a little while of going to Trinity Fellowship with me, she loved it. After we were married, we even started attending the Blended Family group. We enjoyed it so much that we began taking over the Blended Family group, ministering to other families with children from previous relationships.

When I was offered a job in Memphis, Texas, as a sergeant, O didn't hesitate to move, even though it was a three-hour round trip to work for her. We bought a house in Memphis that we wanted to renovate together, a project we hoped would bring us even closer.

But we didn't anticipate how much time we would spend at work or on the house. I was so busy; there were days I was lucky to get an hour of sleep before I had to go back to the station. And with O traveling so much, it felt like we never saw each other.

Our relationship had seemed perfect, but cracks were starting to form. At first, I didn't really pay attention to them, but the larger they became, the harder they were to ignore. And then suddenly, the biggest stressor in our relationship was glaring right back at me in the form of my stepson.

O's son had become too much for her when he was seven. She'd had to make the difficult decision to send him to live with his father because she could no longer control him. It was possibly one of the hardest things she had ever had to do, because she knew how abusive her first husband was, but she felt she had no other choice. Her guilt ate at her.

Her son was having issues at home with his father. He didn't get along with his stepmother, was struggling in school, and he told O that he was frequently being beaten by his dad. I am still unsure if that was the real reason or if his dad and stepmom couldn't handle him any longer and simply kicked him out.

Knowing what I know now, I am more confident they did, in fact, make him leave.

We decided to move to Borger, Texas, in November 2017 to be closer to O's work again and to have her son move in with us. As days turned into weeks, I saw his anger issues up close. Of course, he had been around an allegedly abusive father all of his life and shared DNA with the man. Nature and nurture were both working against this boy, but then again, it is the same story for a lot of people.

That is no excuse for the things this...little shit...has done.

O let him get away with anything at home. Drugs, having a fake ID, and skipping school to the point a truancy officer was getting involved, were only a few of his infractions, and she didn't make him face any consequences. He was constantly dropping my name and my position within the community to get himself out of trouble, and I was catching hell for it at work.

Then one night, we got a call from the night shift sergeant. My stepson had a girlfriend in Stinnett, and while drunk at a party, he decided he wanted to visit her. He stole another boy's truck while under the influence, and he proceeded to take out several power poles, completely totaling the vehicle.

He didn't have a driver's license.

As expected, he was charged with DUI as a minor.

O paid all his fines. When the parents of the boy whose truck was stolen came forward, O then found a way to come up with $16,000 to keep them silent.

I didn't agree with how she was handling things, but he was her kid. And as she liked to remind me, I was living in her house. Something that she mentioned whenever we argued. She owned everything we had as a couple. I didn't feel like I had the right to say anything, even though I was his stepfather, because O continually made me feel like it wasn't my place.

I should have put my foot down then and kicked him out that same night.

Maybe then I would have saved my baby girl from the nightmare that came next.

9

I CAUGHT HEAT AT WORK OVER MY STEPSON'S BEHAVIOR. THE boy was uncontrollable, and his drug use—which had started as just marijuana but had progressed into cocaine—was an embarrassment I was getting tired of having to deal with.

O wasn't prepared to make him face the consequences of his actions. She would ground him, but she never enforced it. He would regularly curse at her, get in her face and scream at her. In all honesty, I think she was scared of him, and that fear, on top of her agonizing guilt over not being there for him when he was growing up, made her think she had to hand him everything.

As I was getting off night shift one morning, M called me and said she needed to speak to me. A little while previous, our daughter had started counseling, something she'd said she wanted to try. M and I had just thought it was the typical stress that most teenage girls seemed to go through. But that day during her session, she finally felt comfortable enough that she admitted what was really going on with her.

While high one night, O's son and one of his friends...*hurt* my baby girl.

Author Disclaimer

This is an ongoing case, so we are ending this chapter here. Because of the nature of the crime, and that it involves a juvenile victim, we feel we cannot give you more details regarding it without harming the case.

What we can tell you:

It is ongoing.

Per what Jason has told us, he was not allowed in the interview when his daughter was being questioned and giving her report. Due to the fact that he had been in the same house when the alleged crime occurred but did not witness the incident, there was talk of Jason being charged with failure to report as he was a police officer at the time.

There have been delays that we do not fully understand nor have we been given a real explanation for. As per Jason, he hasn't been given any real explanation either.

We have just as many questions as you do.

10

As expected, this put pressure on my marriage to O.

I wanted this boy in jail. She would even agree with me when I would tell her what needed to happen, but then she would turn around and coddle her son.

The thing about O is, she hated my daughter. My daughter is so much like her mother, and O didn't like that. But I considered it normal. Stepparents and their stepchildren rarely got along, from what experience I had with it.

Thankfully, my stepson moved out into a house with some friends after graduating early. The house was a party central, though, and I heard drugs were always available there. As time went on, he went through multiple jobs, and every time he lost one, his excuse was, "They cut my hours." But we lived in a small town, and I knew many of the employers he worked for. So, of course, I asked what was going on and why hours were being cut when there were still HELP WANTED signs in the windows.

Each time, they would tell me the same thing. The boy just walked off the job.

The last job he was able to get, he told us he was laid off

due to COVID. One day, I was approached by one of the deputies, asking if I'd seen my stepson, and out of courtesy, he told me why he was looking for him.

The boy had kept the business credit card from his last job, which he'd been fired from—not laid off, as he'd said—and he had been using it to put gas in his friends' cars. He would put up to a hundred dollars in their tanks, and then they would pay him a portion of that money in cash, which was how he was getting by.

O paid off her son's ex-employer so they wouldn't press charges for the credit card fraud.

The money she was spending to keep her son out of trouble was yet another issue putting pressure on our marriage. O had a good job that paid very, very well. But between the trouble she was constantly paying to keep her son out of, her shopping addiction, and all the bills we had, money was tight. When I asked where all the money was going, she would get upset with me and yell that I shouldn't worry about it because it was her money.

Everything we owned was hers. The house, our vehicles...everything. I wasn't on her checking account—but both of her children were. Yet, she had insisted that her name be put on my checking account. It seemed what was hers was only hers, and what was mine was hers too.

Which she held over my head when things would get rocky. If she was angry with me, she would throw at me, "This is my house. That's my truck you're driving!" But when things were good, she would gush, "I love our home. You look good in your truck."

Our sex life was turning nonexistent. Despite how our relationship started, O was becoming more and more withdrawn in the bedroom. One of my turn-ons was I liked to see her in lingerie, but O hated to wear it because her first two husbands made her feel like she was undesirable. But I loved the way she looked in it. The more I would try to build up her confidence, however, the more she would seem increasingly inhibited.

We tried counseling through our church for a while, right before I took the police chief position in Stinnett. Our relationship felt like it was slipping away. I wanted to hold on to it, but nothing seemed to be working. If anything, she made me feel less and less like the man of our household, and I had zero respect at home.

Back when O and I had first started dating, those who knew her well had told me she wasn't a nice person. Most would even go so far as to call her a bitch. I was starting to see just how right they were.

I'm not trying to excuse what I did next. I know I messed up in the worst way.

I just wanted some respect.

To feel like I was wanted and needed again.

11

Disclaimer
Names have been changed to protect the privacy of those involved.

THE GAME ALL STARTED IN NOVEMBER. THAT WAS WHEN I first opened up a Plenty of Fish account. I was on the site for a few weeks, just chatting with several different women, before I went on my first date with Linda.

We chatted through the app for about five days before I drove down to Lubbock, Texas, and met her on her lunch break. This was about two weeks before Thanksgiving of 2020, and we sat and talked in the parking lot during that time, before arranging to meet up after she got off work for dinner. She brought her daughter. Afterward, Linda invited me back to her place to meet her parents, with whom she'd been living since her divorce.

I didn't want to meet her parents, but I felt like she was pressuring me, and I hadn't yet gotten what I wanted. Sex.

Our second date was the Friday after Thanksgiving, November 27. She had a girls' night planned, so I just decided to hang around Lubbock for a little while until she was finished. But during the evening, she called and talked me into meeting her friends. While they were drinking, they all mentioned they were hungry. I was ready to leave, so I offered to get them food to take back to Linda's house.

Once her friends left that night, Linda and I were intimate for the first time.

The following weekend, December 5, 2020, I returned to Lubbock for our third and final date.

This time, I got a hotel room, and Linda spent Saturday night with me. On the way home, I texted her and told her, "Hey, this isn't going to work. We're moving too fast."

I can't remember saying "I love you" to her, or even her saying it to me.

No, I never asked her to marry me.

No, I didn't give her a ring.

And no, there wasn't even any mention of buying a coffeemaker.

Afterward, Linda contacted O via Facebook, but when O mentioned it to me, I told her it was a scam against cops. Because Linda's page looked generic, O believed me and blocked Linda so she couldn't talk to her again.

At that point, Linda was the only woman I'd met in person, but I was chatting with several other women on Plenty of Fish and through the Facebook dating app as well.

One of those girls is the one the world seems to refer to as "FedEx Stefanie" since there were two women with the same name. I never met that particular Stefanie. But I did play more of a game with her. I would joke about things like, "Does Amazon Prime ship wedding dresses/wedding rings? I can mail you one, and you'll be able to pick it up since you will already be delivering them."

That was when she asked, "Do you send every girl you haven't met a ring?"

And I followed up with, "Only the pretty ones."

I never actually bought her a ring, or even a coffeemaker.

In hopes of getting what I wanted, I would string these women along. If they liked something, I liked it too, so they would think we had something in common. Sometimes it worked; sometimes it didn't. If I felt like we had a connection, then we would meet up.

It was during this time that I was also chatting with a woman named Jessica. The two of us never met, never talked about getting married—and once again, no mention of purchasing a coffeemaker—but she did tell me about the video app Marco Polo. On this app, you just pick who you want to send a video to and then record the video, so I never sent the same video to multiple girls.

Actually, I didn't even realize I never said anyone's name in any of the videos until it was mentioned to me by Lonnie during one of our many interviews for this book. I guess it just became a habit not to call the women by name. It helped me not mess up when I was with them. The one time I did mention a woman by name in a video, the world seemed to think she was more special to me than the others, and I guess, in a way, she was.

12

BEFORE I EVEN BROKE THINGS OFF WITH LINDA, I WAS already talking to the Stephanie who lived in Kansas. She was probably the one I met the most often and got to know the best. She was also the one I was most attracted to, except for one other lady whom I met for the first time in January.

Stephanie had five kids, possibly twenty-five cats, and was paranoid that the entire town was against her. If you have followed this story from when it first went viral, then you are aware of what Stephanie's issues are, but I won't mention them here. That is not my story to tell.

We started talking on the dating app around December 5, 2020, while I was still seeing Linda. On December 11, I met Stephanie for the first time.

She was working in Liberal, Kansas, that Friday, which isn't too far of a drive from Stinnett, so I asked her if she would like me to come up and meet her.

Stephanie was excited that I would do that.

We met in the parking lot of where she was working, and we sat in my vehicle talking—well, I sat and listened, because Stephanie talked and talked and talked. Afterward, I drove back to Stinnett, picked up my son, and went home, where he spent the weekend with me since M and I still share custody.

The second time I went to Kansas was the weekend of December 18. She thought I was arriving that Saturday, but I had this feeling she was seeing another guy at the same time, and I wanted to do a little detective work to see if I was right.

During our phone calls, she would always call me from her car so that her kids didn't overhear what we were talking about or interrupt. I thought I had it timed just right to drive by and see if anyone else was parked in her driveway, but she happened to be sitting in her car as I did my drive-by and spotted me. Of course, she called me.

"What are you doing?" she asked as soon as I answered, and I played it off that I came up early to surprise her.

Because of her paranoia that everyone in her town was against her and only out to get her, she asked me to meet her at a cemetery close to her house. She thought no one could see us from where we were parked, but I could tell anyone who drove past could see us easily enough. The whole time we sat there, she seemed nervous. She wanted to hide since she thought the cops would bother her if she didn't. We sat in my truck and talked for a while, but I noticed a farm truck kept circling the cemetery suspiciously. I thought it might be her ex or the other guy I was sure she was also seeing.

Her nervousness didn't stop her from kissing me for the first time that day, though.

I had reserved a hotel room in Dodge City, thinking it was closer to Stephanie's house, but it was actually over an hour away from where she lived. The next morning, I drove back to her place, and the two of us went shopping for her friend's birthday present.

Afterward, we met up with her friend and had dinner to

celebrate the woman's birthday. Once dinner was over, I dropped Stephanie off so she could pick up her car and follow me back to Dodge City. There, we went to a brewery to talk and get a few drinks before going back to my hotel to have sex.

In the following weeks, I saw Stephanie a few more times and even met her kids on several occasions. January 14, 2021, was the last weekend I went to Kansas, and I was ready to break things off. I drove up that day, and we had dinner with her kids. When we got back to her house, something was wrong with my truck door, and her son couldn't open it. Something had caused it to get stuck, and I had to open it hard, shattering the window.

That night I went to my hotel, and Stephanie spent the night with me again. The next morning, she and her daughter went with me to get my window replaced, and then we spent the day together. One of our stops was at Target. As we passed the coffee machines, I mentioned which one I had and that I really liked it, and she told me which one she had been thinking of buying. But there was never any mention of actually buying that one or any other coffeemaker for her.

In truth, I was already moving on to the next player in my game.

13

THAT FINAL WEEKEND WITH STEPHANIE WAS A BUSY WEEKEND for me. Closer to the end of my time with Stephanie, I had started chatting with Tiffany on the Facebook dating app. Of all of the women I chatted with and dated, Tiffany was the one I was most attracted to, even more so than Stephanie.

My plan was to spend the two days with Stephanie, break it off, and then on my way home, stop in Sweetwater, Texas to go antiquing with Tiffany on January 16.

While I was still getting my window fixed, Stephanie called me in a panic to let me know her son had run away, and I drove straight back to her house to help her search for him.

In the early hours of the morning, once he was found, I sat in my truck with Stephanie trying to break it off. One of the reasons I gave her was that I was very allergic to cats, and it seemed every time I came to visit her, she had even more cats at her house. But she kept saying she wanted us to try, that she loved me and wanted it to work between us. In a moment of weakness, I eventually let her talk me into getting a hotel room again, and we spent the rest of the night together.

In all, I got maybe forty-five minutes of sleep before I was on the road back to Sweetwater, which was seven hours away. Every weekend, I would get Friday, Saturday, and Sunday off, so weekends were the best time for me to meet up with Stephanie and the others.

The plan was to meet up with Tiffany in the Walmart parking lot. I got there in time to go inside and buy her a few bouquets of flowers, and then I went out to meet her at her vehicle. We went to lunch, and I made sure we stopped at Sonic to get drinks because she had told me repeatedly during our chats that it was one of her favorite things to do.

We went ax throwing and had dinner that night. It was fun, but we parted ways with nothing more than plans for the following day. The next morning, we had brunch together before going to the bookstore. When I left, we shared what I thought was a sweet goodbye kiss. I wanted more, but Tiffany wasn't ready.

Not long after I started talking to Tiffany on Facebook, I once again started chatting with Candie. At this point in time, I hadn't met Candie. The extent of our relationship had only been a few times chatting via the Facebook dating app. She disappeared for several weeks, and out of the blue, I saw her again on the app in January.

On my way home from Sweetwater on January 17, I drove straight to Amarillo and met Candie for the very first time. We went to dinner while her ex had the kids, rounding out one of the longest weekends of my entire life.

I was running on pure testosterone and adrenaline after the craziness of that extended weekend. My testosterone levels are high to begin with, something I found out about the hard way in June 2020 when I had a stroke. My levels get so high that it thickens my blood and causes clotting. One of those clots happened to travel to my brain, causing the stroke.

Thankfully, it didn't cause any lasting damage, and I recovered quickly.

14

I MET CANDIE IN PERSON FOR THE SECOND TIME THE following day, Monday, January 18, 2021. Normally, that would have been the time I would have needed to attend the city council meeting, but something came up with one of the council members, and it was rescheduled for later in the week.

While I was meeting up with Candie in Amarillo, O thought I was at the council meeting. Candie snapped a picture of us together and wanted to get it printed, so she sent it to CVS from her phone while we had dinner. Afterward, we picked it up, and she gave me a copy to put on my desk at work.

Once dinner was over, I was ready to head home, but she invited me over to meet her kids and her parents. As with Linda, I felt pressured to meet both, but I reluctantly agreed because I wanted to have sex with her. It was at that point that Candie started bringing up how it would be easier for everyone if I just moved in with her and her kids in Amarillo.

That freaked me out more than a little, but I still played along. This was only the second time we had met in person, and that was within twenty-four hours. But I was still in the game, and the prize for me was sex. Laughing it off, I agreed to her plans for us to go to Taos, New Mexico, together the next weekend—something she had brought up before we had even officially met in person.

On January 19, Candie started sending me pictures from O's Facebook, questioning about us being married. She and O had a mutual friend, and this friend had recognized me when Candie had made a Facebook post. I'd denied that I was married to O, but I figured she would try to contact O in some way, and I quickly talked to my wife about it.

I explained to her that I had an informant who had discovered that I was married, and it could make the case blow up if she didn't help me out. If this informant happened to contact her, she needed to tell them that we'd had our marriage annulled, to protect the case I was working on.

When Candie called later that day, she didn't speak to me or anyone I worked with, or even someone I paid to take the call and pretend to be O.

She spoke directly to my wife.

I sent Candie a message on Marco Polo, apologizing for all the confusion regarding my supposed marriage, and she seemed satisfied after speaking to O.

On January 20, I realized O was starting to get suspicious. She kept asking me to put Life360 on my phone so she could track me. After arguing about it for a while, I simply agreed, knowing there was no way around it without causing a fight between us.

That day, I drove down to Candie's house, which happened to be near a Taco Villa. O was tracking me the whole time because she would send me texts, asking why I had stopped at certain places throughout the day. At first, she thought I stopped at Taco Villa.

The entire time I was at Candie's house, O kept texting me, and I knew I needed to get back. But Candie pushed me onto her bed and tried to get me to have sex with her for the first time. I was tempted, but I knew I was already in trouble, because O continued to text me.

The next day, Candie started questioning me about O again.

Candie called me as she was on her way to the police station because she said she wanted to do a ride-along, but really, her stopping by was to test me about my wife. I, of course, panicked. Everyone at the station knew I was married and who O was. Unsure how to get out of this particular situation, I snuck her into the station through the back, but I happened to get caught by the city secretary.

When I didn't introduce Candie to the secretary or a few other people, she got angry.

I took her into my office, and she produced a frame for the picture we had taken and gotten copies of back on January 18. Earlier in the week, I'd taken a picture of that same photo on my desk, and in the background, my Police Officer's Prayer and even a picture of my two children were showing. When she saw that our picture was just taped there, she decided to bring me a frame for it. But when she saw that the picture was no longer where it had been in the photo I'd sent to her, she got even more upset.

Candie wanted to do the ride-along, so I took her for a drive around Stinnett. From what I can remember, we didn't even talk about O again that day, so I assumed we were okay and still going to Taos.

15

Things appeared to be smoothed out, and I picked her up on January 22 for our weekend in Taos. If she still had suspicions at the time, she didn't mention them, so I thought we were good.

We explored some of the tourist spots as soon as we got to Taos, and we started kissing. Things became heated, and we barely made it back to the hotel, where we had sex for the first time.

It was around that time that Stephanie started liking things I was tagged in on the Stinnett Police Facebook page. My assistant chief of police saw that she was liking the pictures I was in and commented jokingly, "Who is this? New girl-friend?" on the posts. To which, some of Stephanie's friends started gushing to her that we were making it Facebook official. I hadn't seen her since the weekend before, but we were still texting, although I was trying to distance myself more and more in hopes she would get the message.

While Candie was showering, I responded to a few texts from Stephanie to keep her from annoying me all weekend.

By the next day, I realized Candie and I had nothing in

common. Although I had drifted so far from God by this time that I couldn't clearly see the road back to Him, I was still very much a religious man. Candie didn't attend church, and that bothered me. On top of that, she continued to push for me to move in with her—after only having met in person six days before. Throughout the weekend, she just seemed to act more and more off, and it was disturbing to me.

I dropped her off at home on January 24, and as I drove back to my own house, I texted her that I thought we were moving too fast and should slow things down. As with Stephanie, I used the excuse that we were too different—she was a cat person, I was a dog person, I was religious, she wasn't—and in this case, it was absolutely true. She called me and we talked, and that was when I informed her I absolutely *would not* be moving in with her.

Candie became irrationally angry and started yelling. I couldn't take her like that, so I hung up.

I got several messages from her on January 25. "You're a lying piece of shit," came in at 9:00 p.m., followed by, "I'm telling everyone." And then the last one was received at 9:08 p.m. that said, "You fucked with the wrong person."

The next day was when she made the post on the City of Stinnett, Texas, Facebook page. It seemed like, within no more than a blink of my eyes, that post went viral, getting shared thousands upon thousands of times. She and Stephanie started talking, and everything escalated from there.

Things began getting crazy fast, and my head was spinning that so many people around the world were commenting on what was going on. But it wasn't until my kids began getting threats that I messaged both Candie and Stephanie to ask them—beg them, if that was what it took—to stop.

That was the last contact I had with either of them.

That same day, I was put on administrative leave at work.

16

I CONFESSED TO O AS SOON AS EVERYTHING STARTED blowing up in my face.

While I was still at work, she called our pastor and his wife, who came over immediately. The three of them talked about what was going on and prayed for guidance. When I got home, O told me that everything was going to be okay. She forgave me and said we would work everything out.

Relieved, I vowed to go back to counseling with her and do whatever else she thought was needed to make our marriage work.

But that was when we started getting inundated with phone calls from the media, talk shows, and everyone in between. People wanted to know my story or tell me what they thought of me or laugh at me. Suddenly, all the attention I was getting wasn't the kind that made me feel good at all. Everyone I loved was now in pain, and it was the one to blame.

O and I went to bed together like normal, and I honestly thought everything was going to be all right, that I wasn't going to lose my wife. We just needed a few days for things to calm down, and life would get back to normal. I just had to have patience and faith that it would all be over quickly.

Then in the middle of the night, O suddenly sat up in bed. Concerned, I asked if she was all right, and she said no. I'd embarrassed her and her family too much. She no longer had faith in our marriage, and she was done.

She told me to get out of our room. I didn't want to push her more, so I didn't argue any further, and I slept on the couch.

The next morning, she came into the kitchen and told me she was going to her parents' for a few days. I had to get out by Saturday. During that time, I could use the truck she had bought, but it couldn't leave the city limits. If it did, she would report it missing and have me arrested for theft.

I couldn't seem to catch my breath. I was losing every-thing right before my eyes, and on top of that, someone had released my home address and phone number on Facebook. All the local police agencies decided that I was in possible danger and put my house on close patrol.

Not long after O left for her parents' house, the city manager called to ask me to come back to the station to discuss the situation. I was met by a Texas Ranger and a member of the district attorney's office. They questioned me, and then the city manager came in to speak to me alone once again.

I knew I had two choices: resign or be fired. At least with resignation, I would be released with an honorable discharge.

As soon as I resigned, the Ranger arrested me for allegedly tampering with a government document—the annulment papers. Fortunately, a family member was able to bail me out so that I didn't have to spend the night in lockup.

When I look back on everything that happened from November to January, I can see that I was being a narcissist the way I played all of those women along. I realize I may not have abused anyone physically, but I did abuse them emotionally by making them think I loved them.

I basked in all the attention they gave me because I wasn't getting any of it at home. But I struggled with breaking it off every time. I got somewhat emotionally attached to them and didn't want to hurt them. Even though I only wanted far, far away from Candie, I still didn't enjoy hurting her or the other women I strung along for all those weeks.

Now, my life is in shambles. But that isn't the part that bothers me the most. I realize I am the only one responsible for what happened to me. It is the destruction of my children's lives that keeps me awake every night. They started getting threats and then bullied by their peers in school—by grown adults on social media!

I hate that I've put my family through so much because of my poor decisions.

My daughter had to be pulled from school to do virtual learning at home due to all this. Her junior year of high school became nothing like she imagined, and that is all on me. I have no words I can give her that can possibly make up for all the chaos I have brought into her and her brother's lives. "I'm sorry" will never heal the hurt I have caused them, as well as the others whom this madness has touched.

I was selfish and even immature. But I swear, from this day on, my only goal is to protect my children.

THE AUTHORS SIT DOWN WITH JASON
FOR A QUICK Q&A

Terri Anne and I also wanted you to hear from Jason Collier directly, in more of an interview format. After discussing it, we both decided that I was the more...shall we say...*diplomatic* of the two of us. As Jason has discovered, Terri Anne tends to go straight for the throat when asking questions. Whereas I will be a little gentler—when I have to be. So, I sat down with him to ask a few questions. I know you all are wondering at this point if he brought me a coffeepot. No, he did not. But we did each have a coffee while doing the interview. For me, an iced caramel macchiato. For Jason, dark roast with two Sweet'N Lows and a splash of sweet cream creamer.

Lonnie Doris (LD): Thank you, Jason, for sitting down with me. Over the course of the last few weeks, I have gotten to know you, and I want to thank you for opening up to me and Terri Anne. I know a lot of what you told us had to take you back to times in your life that were very painful. As I stated on our first phone call, I don't condone you cheating, but I think this story got stretched way beyond the truth. So, with that being said, when did you catch wind that Candie's post went viral and your personal indiscretions were being plastered all over the internet?

Jason Collier (JC): *I started receiving messages on Facebook from my staff at the time, asking, What is going on? So, I checked Facebook and saw her original post. The next day, I saw all the social media posts. I went to work the day after that, worked about a half a day, got called into my boss's office, and was placed on administrative leave.*

LD: As the readers have read in *Texted Lies, Whispered Truths*, you have gone through a lot of emotional trauma in your life, leading up to the internet scandal in late January/early February, 2021. Did you ever seek out help with a licensed mental health counselor?

JC: With the trauma of my parents' death, I dealt with it on my own. A friend of mine told me to just put it away, and so I did and just let other stuff pile on top. Even after the shooting, I just stuffed it away again.

A friend and coworker of mine saw I was struggling, and he went to my chief to help get me counseling. I saw that counselor for about seven months.

O and I went to a Christian marriage counseling couple. They weren't licensed. They were through the church.

I would love to see somebody now, but at the moment, I don't have any insurance.

LD: You mention in the book that you were a momma's boy. What would your mother say to you if she were still here to see what has happened?

JC: That's a tough one. Honestly, I think my mom would embrace me in a hug, tell me she loves me no matter what, but she would also look me in the eye and tell me she was disappointed. She would have told me she and my dad raised me better. And she expects better, but that she loves me, and we would cry together.

All my life, I was always scared of disappointing either of my parents, and I know this would have had her disappointed in me the most. Yet, I feel as if my mom would have been behind me every step of the way as my family and I struggle through this.

LD: After everything the two of you have gone through together, when exactly do you think things within your relationship with O changed the most to make you seek attention outside of the relationship?

JC: I think with everything held over my head, everything that happened with my daughter—and the perpetrator getting the attention for what he had done—I got tired of getting beat down. You can only get beat down for so long, and that's when I decided to step out.

LD: Did the thought of divorce or separating from O ever cross your mind before joining the various dating sites? What stopped you from separating from her?

JC: A lot of the times when O and I would get into arguments, she threw out divorce as a threat. That always hurt. I would always tell her when we reconciled, we don't use that word. She would agree. Then she'd do it again. She kept divorce forms on her computer, so I knew she could do it at any time.

What stopped me was that I loved her. I still love her. I don't understand why—with everything we have put each other through, it makes no sense—but I love her still.

I knew what the final outcome would be. I guess my feelings for her are what stopped me.

LD: What made you decide to set up profiles on the various dating apps?

JC: I just wanted to branch out and see what was out there. I could learn more about someone from a dating app vs. going to a bar. One thing you don't do as a police officer is go out to a bar or drink within the city you work in. Mostly because you don't want the citizens to see you like that. They lose respect for you. Plus, with COVID, there really weren't any bars to go to since they were all closed. The dating apps were more available and easier to use. Also, if you were getting red flags, you could block them and just be done with them.

LD: Did you get a rush out of seeing multiple women at once? Was that your original intention when you started this, to see how many you could date and not get caught?

JC: No, not really. It was actually pretty tough. I was working full time and, at some point, going to college. I don't remember getting a rush. I might have talked to several at once, but the meetings were spaced out.

No, it wasn't my intention at all. I never wanted to get caught. I was just wanting to get attention. If I found someone I connected with, maybe that would spark me to leave O. I was looking to see what options I had out there.

There was one woman I found, and if things had worked out for us, I might have actually left O for her. I was just that into and that attracted to her. But this all blew up before things could progress to that possibility.

LD: Did you have a game plan or exit strategies in your head if something went wrong and you got caught?

JC: Not specifically. But if something came up, I would just think on the fly and do my best to get out of that situation. But no planned-out exit strategy. If something started rubbing me the wrong way, I would just back away and tell them I wasn't ready for a relationship.

LD: You mention in the book going to Stephanie's a day early because you thought she was possibly seeing someone else. You were seeing or talking to other women—why did it bother you if she was?

JC: *At first, we had a really good connection, and I thought maybe this might go somewhere if I gave it a little more of a chance. There were some red flags, but at the beginning, I was able to throw the flags into the back of my mind. But she would—and so would her kids—talk about the other guys she dated before me. She talked about her ex before me all the time. When he found out we were together, he told her he was in love with her. So, I decided to sneak up there to see if she was playing me.*

LD: The text messages you sent were very encouraging of the feelings they were expressing to you. Why did you send the types of texts you did to these women?

JC: *If I found one I liked and we had a connection, it goes back to the earlier question, could it be my way to separate? I regret what I did and that I hurt anyone. If I got them emotionally involved, then it would be easier if they were the one and they were already attached to me. I made mistakes and bad decisions that hurt others, and I hate that. Looking back, that is not the man I am or who I want to be. And it's not the man I want my son to grow up to be. Even other men, maybe they can learn from my mistakes and not have to go through what I'm going through. I strayed from God and sought earthly flesh instead of His guidance. Not that He is punishing me, but this is where I am because of my choices.*

LD: When did you have time and the means to do all of this and still have the energy to be a father, husband, and police officer?

JC: *It was honestly tough. Looking back on it, I have no idea how I did it. It was a lot of physical hours and emotional time invested. I was working twelve hours a day, trying to keep up with being a father and husband. I failed at all of it. I failed as a father, husband, and chief of police. I let them all down.*

Energy-wise, I don't know where it was coming from. I think I'm paying for it now. I am physically and emotionally exhausted. The Devil had a foothold in my life, and when the Devil gets in, he can turn it all upside down.

LD: How did you keep them from finding your personal social media pages—for instance, your Facebook page?

JC: *Prior to starting all of the sites, I went into my Facebook, changed my profile, and made it private. I would tell them it was deactivated or that I didn't go on it. I would tell them that because I was chief, everyone wanted to be your friend, and I just couldn't have it out there.*

LD: If you had the chance to talk to these women again, what would you say to them?

JC: *First off, I'm sorry. I'm sorry for the emotional hurt I caused them and that I know they went into everything with me for a relationship. I am sorry from the bottom of my heart. I know they don't have to forgive me, but I'm truly sorry. I hope for the best for them and hope they move on and find a happy relationship.*

LD: If O showed up at your door tomorrow, saying she was ready to give you another chance, would you take it?

JC: *I'm on the fence. Like I said, I love her. I have seen the woman she became, coming from the lifestyle we were in, seeing her mature, seeing her grow closer to God, which was amazing. But on the other side of the fence, I see the struggles and the things she held over my head and the broken promises she made to me. That causes me to pause on what I would do. I love her, but we would have to seek professional counseling together and individually. And be in agreement that we would work on the hurts we cause each other.*

LD: What is the positive you want to come out of this chaos and mess you have brought into your life and your children's lives?

JC: *I hope that if someone who is growing up, or someone in a strained relationship, looks at my situation as an example and learns from the mistakes I made, it can have a positive outcome. I want people to know there is still hope. They don't have to do what I did to seek attention at home. All they have to do is communicate and seek out help—professionally, if possible. I hope my story can get out there so people can learn. Be encouraged by seeing what my kids are going through, and what I'm going through, not to make the same mistakes I did and see that it doesn't have to be this way if they get help before it gets out of hand.*

LD: You said in the book that you crave sexual attention. Do you consider yourself a sex addict?

JC: *No, I don't consider myself a sex addict because most of what I was craving was the companionship. I enjoyed being with someone in public, walking around with them, and the public displays of affection, holding hands, arms around each other, kissing.*

Sex was a secondary benefit. My craving was just companionship. I have narcissistic tendencies, but I don't see myself as a sex addict.

Terri Anne Browning (TAB): **At the last minute cutting into the Q&A** Hey, sorry to just crash your interview—*Takes a sip of my iced decaf skinny vanilla latte. Hey, it's like 9 p.m. in Virginia, people!*—but I have a question… and just a warning, it may have a follow-up question…or two.

LD: Please do, TA!

TAB: So, Jason, there have been a few women who have stated that you are in a relationship with them and you have kids together. One said you were in Iraq, have been married for a year and have a child. The other said you have been together for three years with a child. However, Candie may or may not have mentioned that you had a vasectomy. Was she speaking the truth?

JC: Yes, she is right. I had a vasectomy in 2012 while still married to my first wife, M. We were done having children, and the doctor explained to us that it would be easier on me to have the procedure than it would be if M had her tubes tied.

TAB: I have a follow-up question. Did you wear protection when you had sex with any of those women?

JC: No...

TAB: Then I definitely have a follow-up question to my follow-up. Have you been tested for STIs and HIV since all of this blew up?

JC: Yes. The same week that everything went viral, I got tested for both, and everything came back negative.

LD: Thank you for taking the time to answer all of our questions, Jason. TA and I have appreciated you taking time from your already chaotic life to sit with us and tell us your story. We realize this must have been very difficult with everything still continuing to be unresolved, but we are thankful you allowed the two of us to tell your story.

Now turn the page to read the debunked lies Jason has been able to set straight for us.

LONNIE DEBUNKS THE LIES

One of the big things I saw come out of the Jason Collier dumpster fire was people coming out of the woodwork with some untruths to be part of this story.

Why?

To be included.

To get some of the attention the original poster was getting.

Only *they* know why they chimed in by posting untruths.

A lot of people were quick to believe what some of these women—and a few men—were posting. Below are a couple "lies" that were eventually debunked. (I'm only using initials of the posters so as to not give them more credit)

Facebook User: She posted on Facebook pretending to be Jason's first wife, stating she was still married to him and wanting some answers.

This was someone just looking for attention—she was not Jason's first wife.

Others came forward on social media, claiming to be married to Jason and the mother of his children, each of them stating that their children were toddler-aged. It may be true that they are, in fact, married to *a* Jason Collier and have children with him, but they are most definitely not married to *this* particular Jason Collier. And since he had a vasectomy in 2012, then had all the tests done to ensure he was no longer able to procreate, he couldn't possibly be the father.

Yet Another Facebook User: She posted on Facebook that she had a friend who had been in a relationship with Jason since she was fourteen years old—FOURTEEN YEARS OLD!

I don't care who you are and what you have done. That is a serious accusation and something that should never be said IF IT'S UNTRUE. *The original poster allegedly posted later she did it to "prove that people will believe anything these days." Still not cool. That post could have opened the door to a whole new set of issues.*

In the weeks following Jason's story, another Jason Collier was arrested. He is forty-four and also lives in Texas —*Nacogdoches County*, Texas, to be exact. After undercover authorities posed as a fourteen-year-old girl, and this particular Jason had been told straightaway of the girl's age on several occasions over the course of their weeklong online friendship, he made plans to meet up with her and was promptly arrested for online solicitation of a minor.

I'm sure most of us played the game Telephone when we were younger. The internet has provided people a new platform to take this game and give it a fresh twist. People were posting just for the sake of posting, it seemed. Jason was even accused of being a part of the disappearance of a missing girl. Her family came out and debunked that. It almost seemed because of this story, the original post that had gone viral, people wanted to hang him out on unsolved cases and other allegations of molestation and inappropriate behavior.

Facebook pages were being created left and right, with

one group topping 200,000 members at one point. For a week in late January/early February 2021, people were coming together to watch this story, watch this man's life fall apart, and even to turn on and attack the two original women at the center of the story.

Even as I sit here and write this, my phone is dinging with text messages of screenshots, because Jason is allegedly back on one of the dating apps. There are fake Facebook profiles claiming they are "Jason Collier," using his picture in their profile.

I'm not here to judge anyone who finds enjoyment in mistruths they post online. I mean, come on, haven't you heard "Online" by Brad Paisley? He spells it out in the song. People can become someone else online; they can become cooler online.

TikTok "stars" were made because of their coverage of Jason Collier's story. Podcasts had record numbers of listeners because they were talking about this, even bringing some of the key players on their shows.

But do you know who wasn't talking?

Jason Collier.

His life, at his own hand—let me make that clear—was falling apart at his feet. He has lost everything except maybe his children and a few family members. Let me reiterate. Does he deserve to lose his wife for cheating on her? *Yes*, a thousand times, yes.

Would you want this brought to your doorstep the way it was brought to his? I mean, really, who hasn't done something they shouldn't have?

It has been proven online, so take that for what it is worth, that Candie has done this before to other men—*married* men —who ended relationships with her. As a woman, I find that doesn't sit right with me, especially for a seven-to-ten-day relationship. She could have simply shown up at his house, told his wife what had been going on, stopped at the store, grabbed some ice cream, and eaten until she was out of her feelings.

She worded her original post to make people believe she had been in a long-term relationship with Jason. What does *long-term* mean to you? It means more than seven-to-ten days to me. But if she would have posted how short the relationship was, I'm pretty confident she wouldn't have gotten the "sympathy" she was seeking. My opinion, but I saw holes on night one.

I guess the good of this story is people made new friends in these groups, one TikTok creator has started a whole series "investigating" current events and went from 1,500 to 89,000 and counting followers—and last but not least, Terri Anne and I got to write our first nonfiction together.

FINAL OPINION FROM THE AUTHORS

Lonnie Doris

My alter ego jumped down this rabbit hole almost immediately upon seeing it shared by a friend of hers and Terri Anne's. But right away, she started shooting holes into the story that was being laid out in front of her. She watched two women go back and forth, seeking attention on whom he "cared" for more. She saw other women coming out with some truths and some made-up stories to get their five minutes. As the days progressed, and more lies came out, her caring and gentle soul wanted to help keep the mean-spirited people away. So, she reached out to Jason—I assure you she told him she didn't agree with him and what he had done, but she also didn't agree with some of the actions by others, trying to make a mockery of him with their evil pranks and antics. Gotta love her; she has a heart, unlike me.

When my alter ego came to me (in my head, of course) to ask me about teaming up with Terri Anne to write this story, I was skeptical. But, in the end, if you know my alter ego, she is convincing, so I said yes. I didn't say yes because I agreed with what Jason had done. Quite the contrary, and we made it clear to him we did not agree or support his actions. I said yes because, before knowing what I know now, I felt there was a story to tell. The original story I thought would be told, based on what I saw unfolding on the socials, was about weight loss and how it can change a person—sometimes not for the better.

But I soon found out, while Terri Anne and I were interviewing Jason nightly for a week, there is so much more to this story. There are so many moving parts that I, quite frankly, was beginning to feel my head spin. And at the end of it, I had to go to my secluded place just to recharge...and so did my alter ego.

Do I still believe Jason's side of the story needed to be told? Yes. Yes, I do. Because, honestly, it's not just about Jason. As you'll read in Terri Anne's statement, it's about his children. My alter ego and I have shed many tears for these children over the course of this story.

By telling this story and with the majority of the proceeds going to them, I know their futures will be bright on the other side of this. I think it says a lot about how Jason feels that his children were hurt by his actions. And by him trying to make it up to them by giving them a better future shows me that he may be redeemable. Maybe? That's on his shoulders, and actions speak louder than words.

I also hope that his story will help someone else.

Terri Anne Browning

As we come to the close of this book, I would like to take a moment and tell you my thoughts on why I decided to agree to write this book.

Writing nonfiction is something that was completely outside of my comfort zone. I feel much more in control of fictional characters that I—*ahem*, attempt—to govern as the story progresses. Turning someone's real-life narrative into something readable was a process I had little power over because I wasn't sitting there talking to the characters who constantly drive me crazy, but an actual, living person who had a story I had zero control in creating.

I'm sure at this point those who have read my other books are wondering what the hell is wrong with me, and why I would put my other books on pause to take the time and even listen to Jason Collier's story long enough to turn his narrative into something worth reading. As we sat down for our nightly calls, at times, I wondered the same thing myself. But in truth, I'm glad I did, because now I'm even more curious about the other aspects of this story.

Not Jason's or Candie's or even Stephanie's. Frankly, I'm finished with these people and their drama. None of them are worth my time now.

Jason's children were—and still are—the reason I agreed to write this short narrative in his words to begin with. A narrative I endeavored to remain impartial to as I wrote it so that my own feelings didn't spill over into his words. As I saw the craziness that was going on via social media, it wasn't hard to imagine what kind of chaos these children's lives must have suddenly become. Just thinking about it broke my heart. Being a mother of three, I couldn't just sit back and stay silent when I had the opportunity to help, even if in a minuscule way.

Then we got to the part where Jason's daughter was... hurt. I wanted to put it in the book, but at the same time, I was reluctant without both her and her mother's permission— plus, there is the whole ongoing investigation to consider. Luckily, Lonnie and I were persistent, because if we hadn't been, Jason wouldn't have told them at all. I very well may have vomited if that had happened, knowing that I was responsible for putting that poor girl through such an ordeal all over again without her permission.

I told him exactly what I thought of him, and I'm sure he is not my biggest fan.

When I learned that neither his daughter nor ex-wife knew about the book or what was potentially going to be published, I felt physically ill. My trust in Jason vanished that day—although it wasn't strong to begin with. And I promised myself, along with his daughter and M, that from here on out, they were now mine to protect. Lonnie and I now have two more honorary members of our family.

Stay tuned. I'm sure you're going to hear more of this story in the future in other aspects.

And from other points of view.

You didn't honestly think this was the end, did you?